First Facts®

Long Ago and Today

FOOD
LONG AGO and TODAY

by Linda LeBoutillier

Consultant:
Daniel Zielske
Professor of Anthropology
South Central College
North Mankato, Minnesota

CAPSTONE PRESS
a capstone imprint

First Facts are published by Capstone Press,
1710 Roe Crest Drive, North Mankato, Minnesota 56003
www.capstonepub.com

Library of Congress Cataloging-in-Publication Data
Linda LeBoutillier
Food long ago and today / Linda LeBoutillier.
pages cm.—(First Facts books: Long ago and today)
Includes bibliographical references and index.
ISBN 978-1-4914-0297-9 (library binding)
ISBN 978-1-4914-0305-1 (paperback)
ISBN 978-1-4914-0301-3 (eBook PDF)
Food—History—Juveline literature. Food supply—History—Juveline literature.
I. Title.
TX355 .L367 2015
641.309   2013050326

Editorial Credits
Nate LeBoutillier, editor; Juliette Peters, designer; Eric Gohl, media researcher;
Tori Abraham, production specialist

Photo Credits
Alamy: North Wind Picture Archives, 9; Capstone Studio: Karon Dubke,
21; Dreamstime: Monkey Business Images, 15; iStockphotos: duncan1890, 7;
Newscom: akg-images, 11; Shutterstock: ER_09, 5, Everett Collection, 1 (left), 13,
Luiz Rocha, 1 (right), Monkey Business Images, 17, mycola, background, pan_
kung, 18, Peter Lorimer, cover (top), Solutioning Incorporated, cover (bottom),
Valentyn Volkov, 20

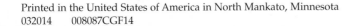

Printed in the United States of America in North Mankato, Minnesota
032014   008087CGF14

TABLE OF CONTENTS

FOOD IN OUR WORLD

Early humans ate whatever food they could find. They ate it right away, so animals wouldn't get it. They moved from place to place to get food. Fire, farming, and raising animals changed everything. Today **technology** gives us more choices of what to eat.

• •

technology—the use of science to do practical things, such as designing complex machines

FOOD IN
ANCIENT TIMES
TO THE 1500S

Early humans gathered fruits, nuts, seeds, and leaves. They **scavenged** meat from dead animals. People grew wheat and baked bread in ovens. Farmers raised animals for meat. Poor people ate bread and cheese or rice and vegetables. Rich people ate meat and fruit. Salt and spices were expensive.

• •

scavenge—to take from what has been left behind

FOOD IN THE
AMERICAN COLONIES
1600S-1700S

American Indians taught the first European colonists to plant corn. Indians also introduced them to pumpkins, squash, potatoes, eggplants, and beans. They also knew where to find nuts and berries. Colonists ate bread, meat, and cheese. They also ate many new kinds of vegetables and fruit. For dessert they ate cakes, puddings, and pies.

FACT:
In early European cities, drinking water often made people sick. Instead people drank wine, beer, or cider.

FOOD ON THE FRONTIER
1800S

In the 1800s **pioneers** going west carried dried meat and beans. They carried flour for **quick breads**. They didn't eat much fresh food until they settled down and grew gardens. Settlers drank water. Milk did not stay fresh. Pioneers used it for making cheese, not for drinking.

• •

pioneer—someone who moves to live in a new land

quick bread—a bread made without yeast including cornbread and banana bread

Texas pioneers in 1880 eating near a supply wagon

FOOD EARLY IN THE 20TH CENTURY

People first used **iceboxes** to keep food fresh in the mid-1800s. Modern refrigerators were first sold in the 1920s. Food was put in tin cans and aluminum foil for soldiers in World War II (1939–1945). Meat, butter, and sugar were **rationed** because there was not enough. People grew "victory gardens" at home for extra food.

• •

icebox—an insulated food box with a block of ice inside

ration—to give out in limited amounts

an early refrigerator

FOOD LATE IN THE
20TH CENTURY

Refrigerators with freezers attached became popular in the 1960s. People bought more frozen, dried, and canned food with **preservatives**. Food was packaged in aluminum and plastic. Young people ate more junk food and fast food. Trucks, planes, and ships brought in new foods from other countries.

• •

preservative—a chemical added to food to keep it fresh

FACT:
Some schools in the United States began to serve hot lunches in 1910. In 1966 some schools also started to serve breakfast.

FOOD TODAY

Today people eat food from anywhere, at any time of year. **Processed food** is made in factories. People read labels to see what is in the food. Organic food is grown without chemicals. Some food is **genetically modified**. Americans have more food choices than any other people in the world.

FACT:
Bees are needed to help grow fruits and vegetables. In 2006 beekeepers noticed that lots of bees were dying. Scientists found that pest and weed killers were killing the bees.

processed food—describes food made in factories using ingredients that are not natural

genetically modified—describes food that is changed to add vitamins or to make it grow faster

FOOD IN THE FUTURE

People will grow more food on less land in the future. They may eat wild grasses or insects. They might get vitamins from skin patches for dinner and breathe in chocolate mist for dessert. The future of food is on the way.

FACT:
Hydroponic gardens grow food using water instead of soil. These may be the gardens of the future.

TIMELINE

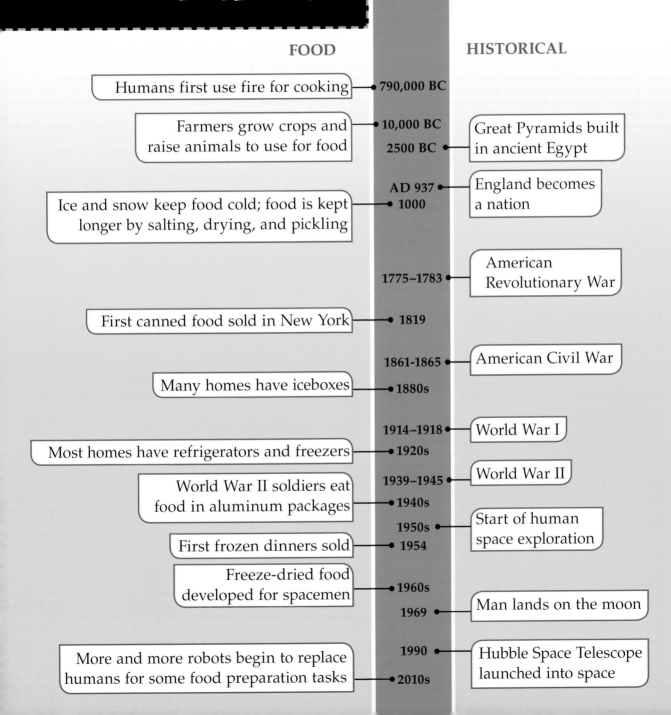

FOOD | HISTORICAL

Humans first use fire for cooking — 790,000 BC

Farmers grow crops and raise animals to use for food — 10,000 BC

2500 BC — Great Pyramids built in ancient Egypt

AD 937 — England becomes a nation

Ice and snow keep food cold; food is kept longer by salting, drying, and pickling — 1000

1775–1783 — American Revolutionary War

First canned food sold in New York — 1819

1861-1865 — American Civil War

Many homes have iceboxes — 1880s

1914–1918 — World War I

Most homes have refrigerators and freezers — 1920s

1939–1945 — World War II

World War II soldiers eat food in aluminum packages — 1940s

1950s — Start of human space exploration

First frozen dinners sold — 1954

Freeze-dried food developed for spacemen — 1960s

1969 — Man lands on the moon

1990 — Hubble Space Telescope launched into space

More and more robots begin to replace humans for some food preparation tasks — 2010s

19

Sweet Treat from the New World

Chocolate comes from cacao beans grown in Mexico and Central America. The Aztec Indians once lived in present-day Mexico. The Aztecs made a thick chocolate drink with chili peppers, cornmeal, and spices in it. Chocolate without sugar tastes bitter. In the early 1900s, Spanish explorer Hernán Cortés arrived in Mexico. Cortés took chocolate back to Europe and he mixed it with sugar and spices. Europeans loved it. The first chocolate bar was made in England in 1847.

Hands On:
BAKE LIKE AN EGYPTIAN

What You Need:
large bowl
cloth
greased baking sheet
1¾ cups (415 mL) whole wheat flour
½ teaspoon (2.5 mL) salt
¼ ounce (15 grams) dry yeast
1 cup (240 mL) water

What You Do:
1. Put flour and salt in a
large bowl.
2. Mix dry yeast with the water.
3. Slowly add the water to
the flour and mix well.
4. Knead the dough with
your hands.
5. Spread the dough on a
clean, flat surface.
6. Roll the dough into small balls.
7. Flatten the balls into round or flat
triangle shapes.
8. Cover the dough with a cloth for
one or two hours, but no longer.
9. Bake the bread on a greased
baking sheet for 30 minutes at
350°F (180°C).

Bread has not changed that much since
it was first baked by the Egyptians.
The first Egyptian bread was flat,
round, and very heavy. They used
only flour and water. Later they
learned to add yeast to their bread.
Yeast causes dough to rise, making
the bread softer and lighter.

GLOSSARY

genetically modified (juh-NET-ik-uh-lee MOD-ih-fide)—describes food that is changed to add vitamins or make it grow faster

icebox (EYESS-boks)—an insulated food box with a block of ice inside

pioneer (pye-uh-NEER)—someone who moves to live in a new land

preservative (pri-ZURV-ah-tihv)—a chemical added to food to keep it fresh

processed food (PRAH-sessed FOOD)—describes food made in factories using ingredients that are not natural

quick bread (KWIK BRED)—a bread made without yeast including cornbread and banana bread

ration (RASH-uhn)—to give out in limited amounts

scavenge (SKAV-uhnj)—to take from what has been left behind

technology (tek-NOL-uh-jee)—the use of science to do practical things, such as designing complex machines

READ MORE

Dickmann, Nancy. *Food from Farms.* World of Farming. Chicago: Heinemann, 2011.

Liebman, Dan. *I Want to be a Chef.* I Want to Be. Buffalo, NY: Firefly Books, 2013.

Olson, Gillia. *MyPlate and You.* Health and Your Body. North Mankato, Minn.: Pebble Plus, 2012.

INTERNET SITES

FactHound offers a safe, fun way to find Internet sites related to this book. All of the sites on FactHound have been researched by our staff.

Here's all you do:

Visit *www.facthound.com*

Type in this code: 9781491402979

Check out projects, games and lots more at
www.capstonekids.com

CRITICAL THINKING USING THE COMMON CORE

1. Page 14 states that people began eating more junk food and fast food in the late 1900s. What do you think led to these changes? (Integration of Knowledge and Ideas)

2. Look at the picture on page 17. Do you recognize some of the foods shown? Where do you suppose this food was grown? (Integration of Knowledge and Ideas)

INDEX